Something In Us

Jeanne Pignoly

Dedication

To my beloved grandmother, Mamie Kaki

To Mother Earth, who carries us and loves us deeply

To all the beautiful souls who need to read these words

Preface

Writing has always been a space where the outside world fades into silence, allowing my soul to speak freely. I have always felt a deep connection with Nature, with the unseen, with the emotions that pass through us like the wind through the trees. Words have accompanied me throughout this inner journey, capturing the essence of my thoughts and feelings, fragments of myself longing to be expressed.

Until now, I have written only for myself. But there is something powerful in daring to offer a part of oneself. Perhaps these spontaneous words, woven from my soul and personal experience, will find an echo within you. Perhaps they will awaken a feeling, a memory, or a question lying dormant within you. These were the words the "past me" needed to read, so perhaps they are what you need to read now.

This collection is an invitation to feel, to explore, to let yourself be moved by the poetry that lives within and around us. It doesn't aim to provide answers, but rather to reflect what sometimes whispers in the depths of our souls.

It makes my heart sing and melt at the same time,
To write spontaneous words that naturally come to me,
To flow into this poetic frequency,
To imagine someone, somewhere, reading my words,
smiling.

To write or not to write?
This is not the question.
Because everything has to be written,
Right?

Acknowledgements

I am deeply grateful to the invisible world that always
supports and guides me throughout my life.

Thank you to my closest friends and family,
Whose unwavering belief in me and love,
No matter the circumstances,
Have been a constant source of strength.

Thank you to Bookleaf Publishing for offering us this
opportunity through this challenge.

A special thank you to my dear friend Inès for her
encouragement and support.

And thank you to the magical Yoga Island in Thailand,
The place where these poems were written and where
inspiration flowed freely.

1. Allow that space to express

There is a magical space in you
That knows,
Truths both vast and subtle.

May you allow it
To speak louder
Until you cannot even quiet it
For the feeling floods your being,
And all you can think about
Is to follow the path this voice is leading.

Don't wonder how to make it happen
Before letting it speak.
Because once it speaks,
You will unfold the impossible
Into a thousand ways revealed.

2. A journey like no other

Can your neighbor, your family, or your country
Understand and validate your choices?
They probably can't,
And you shouldn't worry about it.

Everyone walks their own path,
A path that shifts every moment.
Sometimes light and effortless,
Sometimes winding and unclear.

Do not compare,
Each soul must move through its own experiences.
Cycles change.
Make your own way in the world,
Follow your own rhythm,
Embrace the shifting landscapes :
The emotions, moods, and seasons.

You can only be you.
You could try endlessly
To mirror those you admire
But even if you come close,
It will never shine as brightly
As being the real you.

You were made to be exactly as you are :
With your strange desires,
Your wild dreams,
Your raw beauty,
Your flaws and your fire.
That is the only path
Where you will truly thrive.

3. Insane dreams

Insane dreams
Were planted in your soul
Not just to make you dream,
But to be made real.

They are the fuel, waiting,
To be transformed into matter
To be alchemized into magic.

If such dreams visit your mind
It is a calling to answer,
An invitation to rise,
To bring them to life.

Dreams were never given to you
Only to tease the impossible.
Everything you're capable of imagining,
You're capable of manifesting.

If it's within your heart,
It's within your power.

4. You're the beauty you see

You're dazzled as you gaze upon the mountain,
Adorned by its friend, the sun.

You marvel at your friend's courage,
Honesty, bravery, and radiant spirit.

You're moved by the kindness of a stranger,
Helping another stranger in need.

You're touched by the art and deepness
Of a song, a book, a movie, a dance.

But here's one truth:
You can only see and feel
What already lives within you.
You can't perceive outside
What you don't hold inside.

When your heart melts and expands
For the one you now call your lover,
When you admire the strength, love, or courage
Of people you just met,
It's not something external :
It's you, reflected outward,

Projecting the beauty of your own soul
Onto the world around you.

Every small piece of love you see in others
Is the love that resides within you.
Every act of compassion you offer to others
Is a gift you are capable of giving yourself.

You are it all,
The entire universe in motion.

Be aware to be inside
What you love to see outside,
Because something in you
Already is.

5. Treasured for being

This essence of yours,
That doesn't need to do anything
To be something,
Was, is, and will always be loved,
Treasured,
Simply for existing.

As Nature cherishes
Every fragment of its creation,
You can try to hate, to destroy,
To do the unthinkable,
Yet still,
You will be held in love,
Valued beyond measure
By the one force that is all.

For this force accepts everything,
Nothing is good or bad.
Everything simply is
Experiences, choices,
The exploration of being.

6. The unknowable

To mentally understand
Is to try grasping
The unknowable
With the mind alone.

And yet, you understand
But can you feel it ?

To be knowledgeable;
How impressive it seems,
How much credit it gives you...
But how close does it bring you to truth?
Do you feel it in your bones?
Do you know it with your heart?

Experience cannot be described.
Words will always fall short,
Never enough to make you truly live it.
You must dive,
Feel it in your body,
Let go of the mind,
Drop the knowledge.
Become the dance itself.

This is not an external reward
It is an inner knowing,
A truth that cannot be understood
By those who have not traveled within.

Once you feel it,
You know, deep down.
And when you know,
Belief dies.
There is nothing left to explain.
No more need for words.

It simply is.

7. The corridor of paths

The journey is not a straight path to the divine,
It is made of a thousand winding roads
Through the paradox of being human.

What to do,
What to become,
What to say,
What to silence,
Where to go,
Where to hold back.

A million voices,
A million possibilities.

All you have to do
Is choose.
But even to not choose is a choice.
And no matter how steep the road is,
You can always take another.

Everything keeps moving,
Flowing,
Unfolding,
Forever.

You can try it all,
Without fear of missing
The « right » path
Because there may be no such thing
As a single perfect linear path.

The « now » is the path.

8. Dear Mother Earth

Goddess Nature,
What more is there to say
Than « home »?

She is our first Mother,
Holding us all in her womb,
Asking for nothing in return.
She nourishes us,
Cherishes us,
Accepts us fully.
She is the purest form of compassion.

Dear Gaia,
I love you beyond words.
When I disconnect from you,
I lose myself.
Forgive me
For straying too far.
Forgive us all for
Forgetting you,
Forgetting where we come from.

What was I thinking
When you were always here,

Patiently waiting
For me to come home?

All this time, I thought
I was craving meaning,
When in truth,
I was longing for you
For where I belong.
I am a child of Nature.
That is why I came to Earth,
For you.
To reveal your beauty,
To help others hear your heartbeat again.

I love you so much
That it aches
To realize that sometimes
I can speak of you
Without truly *feeling* you.
Because when we deeply connect to you,
Nothing else matters.

You are so perfectly beautiful
That if we truly saw you,
If we truly listened,
We would find,
Individually and collectively

The courage
To love, protect, and care for you
As you have always cared for us.

9. The Sun in Someone's Life

Something in you,
Is lighting up someone's life,
Even when you don't know it.

If you can't shine for yourself,
Shine for others.
Shine for the world.
Because you are the world.

Never forget:
You are a reflection of someone's beauty,
You are the version someone aspires to be,
You are the inspiration for someone to act.

And that alone,
Is reason enough to keep showing up,
To keep trying, keep hoping,
To trust that better days will come,
To know that you are capable
Of everything you have ever dreamed of.

You are always inspiring someone
To do, to be, to smile, to hope or to act.

Even when you don't see it,
You are the sun in someone else's life.

And if you can inspire others
You can inspire yourself.
If they see light in you,
It is truly within you.

10. You are I and I am You

The other is part of you,
You are part of the other.
When you hurt yourself,
You hurt others.
When you love others,
You love yourself.

Yet, to only think about yourself
Is a partial understanding.
Only through being
A pure, compassionate heart,
Only through giving naturally
For the act of giving itself
Can you truly feel what it means,
To love and to be loved.

Yet, to only think about others
Is a partial understanding.
Only through honoring
Your inner being, values and calling,
Only through listening to your intuition
And gently asserting your needs,
Can you truly feel what it means
To be aligned and yourself.

It's all in the balance:
Giving and Receiving,
You and the other,
Same and same,
Mirroring
The same Source.

11. Divinely betrayed

Just betrayed
By the people you loved and trusted the most,
You collapse in shock,
Crying out at the injustice.

First, doubt sets in:
You question who you are, your kindness,
And your very existence.
Then, as the weight of injustice settles,
A fleeting thought of revenge crosses your mind,
A natural urge to restore balance
To the unfairness you never deserved.

The pain feels immense and overwhelming.
There seems to be no reason for it,
As you were always trying your best,
Always offering your love.

What if...
The betrayal was necessary,
To redirect you toward a more aligned path?
What if...
The betrayers were not the central force,
But only characters in a larger scheme,

The divine, cosmic game of life?
What if...
Deep down,
Something in you already knew this was meant to
happen,
That it all unfolded for a reason?
What if...
What feels like a tragedy right now
Is actually your greatest hidden blessing?

Take a step back. Break the cycle.
Rise higher. Choose differently.

Embrace it. Forgive. Heal. Move forward.

Learn from the lessons it carries,
Because this was not just betrayal,
It was divine intervention in disguise.

12. Unconditional Love

Not a single moment or act of love is ever wasted.
Love is love.
Attachment is not love.
To love unconditionally is to love
Fully, completely,
No matter the conditions.

It means loving even when
There's nothing to receive in return,
Even when no story is possible,
Even when they have betrayed you.
Because love is beyond actions and words,
Beyond right and wrong.

Love always carries good intentions,
Even when actions sometimes go wrong.
The purity of love remains untouched,
Unbreakable, eternal.

This is who we all are at our core,
But we can only realize it
When we let go of identifications,
Expectations,
And the stories we tell ourselves.

It is a matter of awareness,
Of consciousness.

13. The Devil in you

Ooh, big time.
That "something" in us,
Could it sometimes be
The devil's strategies,
Emerging from another space,
Trying to recruit us,
To hurt those we love most?

Really?
A force taking the reins,
Stealing power from you
Without you knowing?

Darling,
You are your own master.
You're not fighting devil forces.
You're avoiding your own reflection,
Your patterns,
Your shadows,
A natural part of this human experience.

It's not a big deal.
Stop fighting, stop fearing.
Start choosing.

Start acknowledging.
Let it all flow naturally.

But first, you must accept:
To be human.
To be ego-driven,
To be beautifully and chaotically flawed.

It was always your own darkness speaking.
The moment you see it,
Work with it,
And embrace it;
That's when fear fades.
That's when the shift begins.

When you boldly break free
And dare to believe differently,
See differently,
Listen differently,
Then,
Your deeper journey can begin.

14. Dance with your heart

Let your body fully immerse
In the rhythm and the notes.
Feel the beat with your soul,
Observe your whole being
Moving to the frequency
Without you ordering it.

Dance the way your body makes you dance
Let it take you to a space of magic,
Where you taste the sweetness of the divine.
Let it guide you into a realm of bliss
Where no performance is needed.

When the mind dissolves,
And the effort fades,
Movement happens on its own.
Led by your inner knowledge
You become the dance
And the dance becomes your teacher.

Dance to celebrate
Dance to express
Dance to release
Dance to heal

Dance to dance

Open your heart to the dance,
Feel it fill you.

15. Life is your lover

Even when life breaks you,
Never stop loving,
Because love is life.
It is what we are made of.
It is the only nourishment
That truly fills us.

Live and embrace
Every form of love,
For love is universal,
Not just found in a lover.

How lucky are those
Who understand this truth,
They will never feel unloved again.

Love is everywhere:
Love is in your grandmother's meals.
Love is in the shelter of a tree.
Love is in the pure intention of a child.
Love is in a friend's quiet act of service.
Love is in the words of a letter sent with care.
Love is in a whispered thank you.
Love is in a selfless gesture.

Love is in the smile of a stranger.

Love is in everything,
For those who keep their hearts open.

16. Drop the fight

To live we have learned to fight:
Fight to be accepted, to be loved, to survive.
Fight against society, against our flaws, against darkness.

But the new world lies
In the acceptance of all that is.

How can we create a new society by fighting?
How can we become a better person by resisting?
Fighting creates separation,
Fighting fuels confrontation.

Only when we accept can we start
Building,
Creating,
Alchemizing,
Becoming.

But first,
We must accept.
Accept our patterns,
Accept our conditions,
Accept our sadness,
Accept the injustice,

Accept the seasons,
Accept the world.

17. Our friend the wind

Have you ever thanked our friend, the wind?
It comes and caresses our skin,
A gentle whisper felt within,
Reminding us we are part of a greater scheme.

On its way,
It carries the untold stories of the world.
It makes the leaves and our hair dance
With freedom and lightness.

It embraces us softly,
Then takes away
All that we no longer need,
Moving the energy
To another place.

If you listen closely,
You can even hear its teachings
And get inspired
By the natural wisdom,
Only it can share.

18. Awareness of the whole

How insanely beautiful it is
To know that
The entire universe is within you.
To know that
No matter what is happening outside,
In the constant drama of life,
It changes nothing inside.

You are and you will always be
This entire universe on your own.
You gotta remember it,
You gotta make an effort
To acknowledge it
Before losing touch with it.

And yet,
I don't even know why I'm writing about it,
Because every minute I forget about it.

But something in me knows that
It's a choice of every moment,
A constant work,
A path paved with hardships,

But this is the only way out:
Awareness of the divine within us.

19. Your own guru

Never give your power away.
Something in you
Knows exactly what is right for you.

Your heart is your compass,
Your body is your guide,
Your joy is your thermometer.

Life is your teacher,
Nature is your mentor,
Intuition is your guru.

Be courageous enough
To listen to the sound of your inner voice.
Don't escape into someone else's advice
If you are truly honest with yourself,
You will always know
What is best for you.

Even when things don't seem to make sense
And you're searching for answers,
Trust that everything will unfold how it should.

The feelings of a hundred people

Will never be better for you
Than your own gut feeling.

It's your journey, your life,
Make your own decisions.

20. The transition of Death

Death is not the end,
It is a transition.

Yet, it is the death of your personality,
And of your human character.
It is frightening for the ego,
Unbearable for the mind,
But it is natural for the soul.

Fear not, for it is the inevitable process
Of this journey we all share.
Honor it, and let it remind you
To cherish each second fully,
To never miss a single minute
Of this fleeting life you have.

It is the only moment you will ever have
As you are, in this specific human form.

When death arrives,
You will be ready,
As the tree is ready to shed its leaves,
When autumn comes.

21. Silence

Silence can be noisy,
Full of thoughts.

Silence can be tense,
Full of grudges.

Silence can be meaningful,
Full of emotions.

But most importantly,
Silence can be full of presence.

And only in silence
Can total awareness be found.

It is only there
Where reality becomes real.

It is where it all begins :
In silence.